W9-CGP-218

MEXICO

Maps Matthews & Taylor Associates, pages 46 and 47

Contents page: Aztec musicians at a festival.

Photographic sources Key to positions of illustrations (T) top, (C) center, (B) bottom, (L) left, (R) right.

A.G.E. illustración: 8 (B), 13 (BR), 17 (T). Associated Press: 35 (BL). The Bettmann Archive: 17 (BR), 18–9 (B), 19 (BR). Bodleian Library: 10 (L). British Museum: 15 (TL). Camera Press: 12 (TL), 20 (CL), 20 (TR), 29 (TR), 33 (TL). M. Casasola: 19 (TL), 19 (TR). Cement and Concrete Association: 33 (TR). Counselate General of Mexico: 21 (TR). Culver Pictures: 18 (TL), 18 (BL), 19 (CR). Giraudon/Art Resource: 15 (BR). Robert Harding Associates: all photos by Robert Cundy except where stated; 20 (BL), 21 (TL); 25 (BL): photo Sybil Sassoon; 26 (BR), 27 (BR): photo John Gardy; 29 (BR), 31 (BR), 39 (TL), 42 (TL). Leo Hetzel: 20 (TL), 43 (TR). Keystone: 15 (CL). Magnum Photos/Alex Webb: 21 (BR). Mexico Government Tourism Office: 22 (TL), 34 (BR). Dennis Moore: 8 (T), 9 (BL), 9 (BR), 11 (BR), 13 (TL), 22 (BL), 22 (R),

23 (TR), 23 (BR), 24 (TR), 25 (TR), 25 (CL), 27 (TL), 30 (TR), 31 (TL), 31 (TR), 32 (B), 33 (BL), 35 (TR), 35 (TL), 36 (TL), 37 (TL), 38 (BR), 39 (B), 41 (BL), 42 (BL), 42–3 (B), 43 (CR), 43 (BR). Spectrum: 41 (TR). Picturepoint: 16 (B). Productions TéléVision Rencontre: 11 (TL), 12 (BR). Reuters/Bettmann: 30 (BR). SEF: 12 (BL), 39 (TR), 41 (TL). Ronald Sheridan: 40 (BR). UNICEF/Didier Bregnard: 43 (TL). Woodfin Camp/Karl Muller: 41 (BR). ZEFA: 11 (BL), 13 (BL), 15 (TR), 23 (BL), 25 (BR), 26 (T), 27 (TR), 27 (BL), 28 (TL), 28 (BL), 29 (TL), 29 (CL), 29 (BL), 31 (BL), 32 (T), 33 (BR), 34 (TR), 35 (TL), 35 (BR), 37 (C), 38 (TL), 38 (C), 38 (BL), 40 (TR).

©Macdonald & Co (Publishers) Ltd 1976. Revisions © 1991 by Silver Burdett Press, Inc.

First published in Great Britain in 1976 by Macdonald Educational Ltd.

Published in the United States in 1977 by Silver Burdett Press, Morristown, N.J.

Revised 1991 by Silver Burdett Press, Englewood Cliffs, N.J.

Library of Congress Cataloging-in-Publication Data

Howard, John.

Mexico / John Howard.—Rev. ed.
p. cm.—(Silver Burdett countries)
Rev. ed. of: Mexico, the land and its people
Includes bibliographical references and index.
Summary: Discusses the geography, people, history, culture, and other aspects of Mexico.
1. Mexico—Juvenile literature.
[1. Mexico.] I. Title. II. Series.
F1208.5.H68 1991
972—dc20
ISBN 0-382-24247-5   91-18013
                                          CIP
                                          AC

Cover photo: Mexico Government Tourism Office

REVISED EDITION

SILVER BURDETT COUNTRIES

MEXICO

John Howard

SILVER BURDETT PRESS

Contents

A land of many faces

An extraordinary landscape

Mexico curves southward from the United States border to the Central American countries of Guatemala and Belize. Its shores are washed by the blue waters of the Pacific, the Caribbean, and the Gulf of Mexico, from which the Gulf Stream flows.

Mexico is a land of snowcapped mountains and volcanoes, high plateaus, and tropical rain forests. Arid deserts contrast with placid lakes and green plantations. Its coastline and land borders extend over 8,700 miles (14,000 kilometers), enclosing a country about three times as large as Texas.

Highest of all the snowy mountain peaks is the perfect cone of Pico de Orizaba, worshipped by the ancient Indians as the "Mountain of the Star." Rising above the Valley of Mexico is Ixtaccíhuatl ("The Sleeping Woman"). Watching over her nearby is her sentinel Popocatépetl ("The Smoking Mountain").

Deserts and jungles

Most of the desert country is in the north and west, but hundreds of thousands of acres of parched wastelands have been transformed into green and highly productive irrigation zones. In contrast, the Gulf coast and humid jungles of Tabasco are drenched by torrential rains and battered by fierce hurricanes. Yucatan is a flat limestone peninsula that for thousands of years has been the home of the Native Americans called Maya.

The sun shines brilliantly all over Mexico, but the temperature depends very much on the altitude. The central plateaus, known as the *altiplano*, have a benign climate due to an average height of more than 6,500 feet (2,000 meters). The concentration of population in this favored region reflects the enjoyment of warm days and cool nights by more than 40 million Mexicans.

▲ Native legend says that when the volcano Popocatépetl rumbles and smokes, he is mourning for his dead sweetheart, the dormant volcano Ixtaccíhuatl. According to an old story, they were originally a Chichimeca prince and a Toltec princess forbidden to marry. The princess died of a broken heart.

▼ Guadalajara is the second largest city of Mexico and retains much of its old colonial atmosphere. It is famous for its *mariachi* music, animated street life, and enormous Libertad market. The climate is warm. Its Tlaquepaque district is one of Mexico's best centers for pottery and glass.

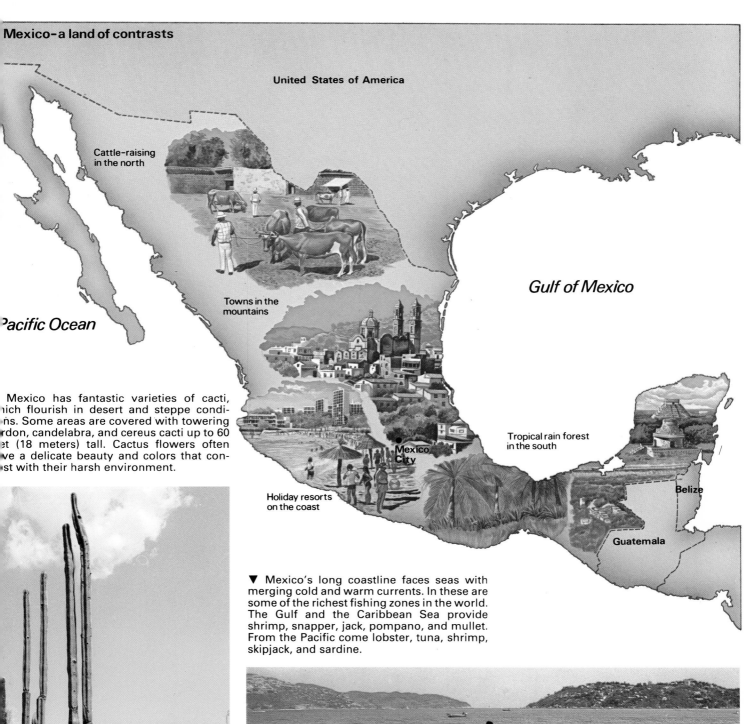

United States of America

Cattle-raising
in the north

Gulf of Mexico

Towns in the
mountains

Pacific Ocean

Tropical rain forest
in the south

Mexico
City

Belize

Holiday resorts
on the coast

Guatemala

Mexico has fantastic varieties of cacti,
hich flourish in desert and steppe condi-
ns. Some areas are covered with towering
rdon, candelabra, and cereus cacti up to 60
et (18 meters) tall. Cactus flowers often
ve a delicate beauty and colors that con-
st with their harsh environment.

▼ Mexico's long coastline faces seas with
merging cold and warm currents. In these are
some of the richest fishing zones in the world.
The Gulf and the Caribbean Sea provide
shrimp, snapper, jack, pompano, and mullet.
From the Pacific come lobster, tuna, shrimp,
skipjack, and sardine.

The people of Mexico

► Before the arrival of the Spaniards in 1517, Europe was ignorant of the existence of the Native civilizations that had flourished for thousands of years in the Americas.

▼ While searching for a place on which to found Tenochtitlán, the Aztecs saw an eagle devouring a snake on a cactus branch and took it as a sign from the gods. The emblem appears today on the Mexico flag.

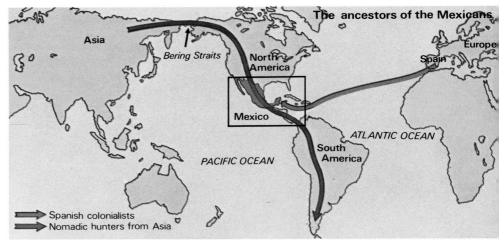

The ancestors of the Mexicans

→ Spanish colonialists
→ Nomadic hunters from Asia

Nomadic hunters

The first people to live in Mexico arrive about 20,000 years ago. They were no madic hunters who crossed the Bering Straits from Asia during the Ice Age when the continents were still connected.

By about 5000 B.C. the first settlers i the valleys and coastal plains began t cultivate maize, beans, and pumpkins The earliest civilizations developed i the center of Mexico about 1800 B.C.

Different tribes traveled across th country, and trade in food and craft wares began. The Olmecs, notable fc their gigantic carved stone heads, settle near Veracruz about 1500 B.C. an strongly influenced the spread of civili zation.

Indian and Spanish empires

Other Indian civilizations that bega their cultures about this time were thos of the Maya in Yucatan and the south east, the Zapotecs around Oaxaca, an the magnificent city-state of Teotihua cán on the central plateau. Empires an dynasties rose and fell, until the warlik Aztecs founded their capital Tenoch titlán in 1325 A.D. on the site of moder Mexico City.

Hernán Cortés landed at Veracruz o April 21, 1519. After many fierce strug gles he captured Tenochtitlán and raze it to the ground. The last Aztec rulers Moctezuma and Cuauhtémoc, wer killed; their empire was destroyed. Th Spanish governed Mexico until the Wa of Independence freed the country i 1821.

The Mexican population today con tains people of European, Native Ameri can, and mixed descent.

A giant stone head carved by the Olmecs. The Olmecs were one of the earliest culture groups of ancient times. They worshipped jaguar, snake, and bird deities who demanded human sacrifices to ensure fertility. The Olmecs developed astronomy and mathematics, and they were potters and sculptors of genius.

The Mexicans today

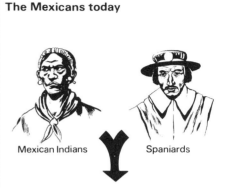

Mexican Indians   Spaniards

▲ About 55 percent of all modern Mexicans are of mixed Spanish and Indian blood and are known as *mestizos*.

◀ The Plaza of the Three Cultures in Mexico City. A housing project in the old part of Mexico City included a site that contained both the Aztec ruins of Tlatelolco and the beautiful Spanish Colonial Church of Santiago. Architect Marío Pani had the new Foreign Ministry built in the same ancient plaza. By this imaginative plan he preserved together three distinctive cultural landmarks.

11

Ancient civilizations

▲ This majestic temple called the Castillo is part of the enormous archeological site of Chichén Itzá in Yucatan. It was built between A.D. 800 and 1200.

▼ The painted walls of Bonampak, remote in the Chiapas jungles, were revealed by the dwindling band of Lacandon Indians, descendants of the Maya. These frescoes are masterpieces of the ancient world.

Long before the arrival of the Spanish in 1519, a succession of civilizations rose and fell, perhaps beginning about 1500 B.C. with the Olmecs. Their culture centered round La Venta, near modern Veracruz. They were pyramid builders and were notable for their delicate figurines and bowls shaped like animals and people. They carved enormous stone heads in the jungles.

The Zapotecs settled in the warm valleys of Oaxaca, assimilating much of the culture of the Olmecs. Monte Albán became their principal center. Excavations have revealed scores of elaborate tombs, plazas, an immense ball court, and many vast temples. Following a collapse of the Zapotec regime, the Mixtec people moved into the area, practiced fine craftsmanship in jade, onyx, silver, and gold, and built the lovely religious center of Mitla.

The Maya inhabited the Yucatan, southern Mexico, and part of Central America. Their formative period began about 1500 B.C., and the peak of their advanced society lasted from about A.D. 400 to 900. They built many magnificent centers such as Palenque, Tikal, and Chichén Itzá, architectural and sculptural masterpieces. The Maya were skilled astronomers and developed a calendar system more accurate than our own.

In the great valley of Anáhuac the Mexica people founded fabulous Teotihuacán ("City of the Gods"), where huge pyramids and temples line the majestic Avenue of the Dead.

The Toltecs, builders and warriors, founded their great capital Tula in the 9th century. The glory of Tula is the now-restored House of Tlahuizcalpantecuhtli ("Lord of the Dawn") and its mighty columns of Warriors of the Sun.

The last great Indian state was that of the Aztecs, who founded Tenochtitlán in A.D. 1325 on an island in Lake Texcoco. It grew rapidly over reclaimed ground and became the capital of a vast empire. The Spanish marvelled at the size and magnificence of what was perhaps then the largest city in the world—but they did not hesitate to destroy it.

▲ This Zapotec funerary urn came from a tomb in the great ceremonial center Monte Albán, near Oaxaca. The richly decorated figure bears the masks of an eagle and a jaguar, showing Olmec influence. It dates from about A.D. 300. Magnificent treasures of gold and jade have been discovered here.

▲ This picture from a Mixtec codex (plural: codices) shows a priest piercing the nose of an official so he can wear his ceremonial jade bar of office plugged through this nose. Elaborately designed gold ornaments like earrings were also worn in this manner.

▲ The pyramids of Teotihuacán are near Mexico City. The Pyramid of the Sun is 215 feet (66 meters) high and was built about 2,000 years ago. It was originally crowned with a statue of the sun god.

◄ The giant "Warriors of the Sun" supported the roof of the vast Toltec temple of The House of the Lord of the Dawn at Tula. From here the legendary Quetzalcóatl, the plumed serpent god, ruled earth and sky.

► The Mixtecs recorded their history on exquisitely painted books called codices, made of long strips of beaten and folded fiber paper. Few specimens of this form of pictographic writing survived the Spanish conquest.

▼ This brilliantly colored mural painting in the Municipal Palace of Mexico City depicts ancient Tlaxcala. The people of Tlaxcala helped Cortés defeat the Aztecs and were the first Native Americans to become Christians.

▲ A Mixtec chief called Eight Deer was involved in dynastic wars for control of an empire. He is shown capturing a nine-year-old relative, Four Wind, who because of his youth was spared the customary death under the sacrificial knife.

The Spanish conquest

▼ Hernán Cortés landed at Veracruz on April 21, 1519, with a small force. On the long march to Tenochtitlán, they were joined by Totonac and Tlaxcalan Indians who were hostile to the Aztecs. Only after long sieges and heavy losses did the Spaniards conquer the city on August 13, 1521.

Arrival at Tenochtitlán

Hernán Cortés landed near Veracruz on Good Friday, 1519, with a small force of 555 men and 16 horses. He led them through fever-ridden jungles and icy mountain passes to the Aztec empire's fabulous capital city, Tenochtitlán.

The Emperor Moctezuma believed that the pale-faced Spanish were of divine origin and received Cortés and his men as honored visitors. The wily Cortés imprisoned the emperor by a trick and became master of the city. But when he returned to Veracruz, his lieutenant, Pedro de Alvarado, murdered some of the Aztec hostages. The people rose in a fury, but Cortés managed to get back to lead the Spanish out of the besieged palace after Moctezuma was killed.

The last Aztec emperor

The following year Cortés mustered h troops and stormed Tenochtitlán. Afte weeks of desperate fighting, the valian new emperor, Cuauhtémoc, surren dered. The city was razed to the ground and Cuauhtémoc was executed in 152 after terrible tortures.

The Viceroyalty

As soon as the Spanish established the rule over "New Spain," exploration colonization, and exploitation of th country began. In 1535 the first vicero Mendoza, arrived from Spain. All au thority was vested in the Crown, and council was instituted to take respons bility for legislation. The Spanish bor in Mexico, called Creoles, were never a lowed any significant part in the govern ment of the country.

Although the kings of Spain desire that the Indians should be protecte from cruelty and exploitation, cond tions for the natives were often harsh many of them lived in poverty and serv tude. Some of the earlier friars sent ou from Spain worked to protect and teac the Indians, but as the Church in Mexic became increasingly rich, it became in different to their suffering.

Fatal epidemics

Imported European diseases such a smallpox decimated the population, an agricultural production fell. Fertile lan was abandoned, leading to the creatio of enormous estates called hacienda with a peonage system of labor that wa really slavery.

The production of the mines assure the Spanish treasury of a prodigiou flow of silver and gold. Aristocrati mine owners lived in huge palaces an entertained on a princely scale.

At the end of the 18th century, th Creole leaders of society in New Spai began to want a greater share in goverr ment. They bided their time for an op portunity to get rid of the Spanish mas ters and create a free Mexico.

The conquest of Mexico

ATLANTIC OCEAN

GULF OF MEXICO

Villa Rica de la Veracruz

Tenochtitlán

Cholula Tlaxcala

Tabasco

YUCATAN PENINSULA

CUBA

CARIBBEAN SEA

← Route of Cortés 1519

◄ Tenochtitlán was perhaps the largest ci in the world at the height of its glory. Th Spanish were overwhelmed by the splende of its huge temples, palaces, and unique floa ing gardens glittering in the center of Lak Texcoco. A Spanish officer, Bernal Díaz, lat wrote an account of the conquest and sai "Never had they ever seen such marvels."

◀ Diego Rivera's murals represent the Spanish as the cruel oppressors of gentle and innocent natives. His work adorns many public buildings in Mexico.

◀ When Cortés first landed on the Mexican coast, he received a gift of some Native women, one of whom, called Malinche, became his interpreter. She accompanied him to Tenochtitlán and is pictured talking with Cortés to an Aztec ambassador.

▼ Morelia, capital of Michoacán State, is the most beautiful and best preserved of the large colonial cities of Mexico. It has a superb cathedral and many handsome old buildings of soft pink stone, like this convent with its dignified patio.

▶ An 18th-century painting of a city square in Mexico shows the different classes of colonial society, which was structured like a pyramid. At the top, with the greatest degree of social status, were aristocrats and priests who had been born in Spain. Next came Creoles, or people of Spanish blood born in Mexico. The middle of the pyramid was made up of mestizos, or people of mixed Spanish and Native American descent. They were often granted some social status, especially if their skin was light. At the base of the social pyramid were the Indians, many of whom were little better off than slaves. Some Indians in remote jungle and desert regions, however, never submitted to Spanish authority.

Independence and the Republic

The Liberty Bell

On September 16, 1810, Father Miguel Hidalgo, parish priest of the little town of Dolores, rang his church bell and shouted to wildly cheering people, "Viva Mexico! Death to the Spaniards!" Within a few days the rebels had taken many cities and controlled large areas of the country. After ferocious massacres and cruel retaliation by Royalist forces, Hidalgo was captured and executed.

Another priest, José María Morelos, joined the rebels and became their leader. He presided over a Congress at Chilpancingo in 1813, affirming democratic government. Then he too was captured and put to death.

A young and unscrupulous Creole soldier, Agustín de Iturbide, then obtained the support of the rebels and triumphantly entered Mexico City in 1821. As Spain refused to recognize an independent Mexico, Iturbide had himself crowned as Emperor Agustín I. His profligate reign ended within a year when he was forced to abdicate. A new Congress elected General Guadalupe Victoria as the first President of the Federal Republic in 1824.

▲ The little town of Dolores Hidalgo was the home of parish priest Miguel Hidalgo. Hidalgo rang the church bell and signalled the start of the 11-year struggle to win independence from Spanish rule.

◄ General Antonio López de Santa Anna was a vain and unscrupulous politician-soldier. His periods of incompetent rule ended in exile and disgrace after the sale of Texas and a disastrous war with the United States.

▼ When the United States integrated Texas with the Union in 1845, Mexico declared war. Cerro Gordo was one of the battles fought before American forces took Mexico City and peace was declared on February 2, 1848.

Bankruptcy and reform

The poverty and unsettled state of the new republic led to a long period of violent instability. Futile governments became involved in disastrous wars with Texas and the United States; Mexico ceded Texas, Arizona, New Mexico, and California to the Americans. The new republic became bankrupt.

Benito Juárez, a great figure in Mexico's history, became president in 1861. He crushed the brief French-backed reign of an Austrian archduke named Maximilian, and he began the task of reconstructing the shattered country. Worn out by the struggle, he died in office in 1872.

In 1876, Porfirio Díaz seized power. The long dictatorship of Díaz restored order and progress, but the Indians and the poor were denied liberty and land.

President Benito Juárez was the greatest figure of the reform period after Independence. A Zapotec lawyer and dedicated patriot, he had the task of reorganizing a war-shattered and bankrupt country. He died of a heart attack in 1872, worn out by his incessant labors.

▼ The Hapsburg archduke Maximilian, brother of the Austrian emperor Franz Joseph, accepted the crown of Mexico after a French military invasion. Bitter strife led to his betrayal, capture, and execution at Querétaro on June 19, 1867. His wife, Carlota, became insane and died in Europe.

▲ Porfirio Díaz controlled Mexico for 34 years. It was a long period of peace, order, and progress—for which the price was heavy. A mestizo from Oaxaca, Díaz was brave, intelligent, cunning, and ruthless. He stabilized the country's finances and encouraged foreign investment. But the Indians and peasants lived in misery, and liberty was abolished. Revolts in the north sparked the Revolution, which led to Díaz's fall and exile to Paris, where he died in 1915.

The Revolution

Madero's presidency

The Mexican Revolution started on November 20, 1910. Francisco Madero, a member of a wealthy Creole family, an idealist and humanitarian, opposed the Díaz regime and was put in prison. Díaz underestimated Madero's popularity and released him, and rebellions began simultaneously in several parts of the country. Mexico joined rebel forces in the north commanded by the former bandit Pancho Villa, while Emiliano Zapata led peasant raids on the rich *haciendas* in the south. Díaz fled the country on May 26, 1911, and on November 6 Madero took over as president.

Madero, a sincere democrat, was not tough enough to control the unruly Congress. The treacherous General Victoriano Huerta then staged a coup, imprisoned Madero and his vice-president Suárez, and made himself president. Madero was assassinated while in custody, and Huerta began a dictatorship that triggered fierce resistance all over the country.

More assassinations

Civil war raged until Venustiano Carranza was able to issue a new constitution on February 5, 1917. It remains the basis of Mexican government today. Soon afterward Carranza became president, but his administration failed to make enough reforms and he was overthrown.

Álvaro Obregón became the next president on December 1, 1920. He established measures of agrarian reform, worked to improve Mexico's economic independence, and launched an educational program.

Plutarco Elías Calles succeeded Obregón as president in 1924. Their two regimes were a consolidation of the Revolution. Calles amended the Constitution to allow Obregón to succeed him for a second term of office in 1928, but Obregón was assassinated at a victory banquet in Mexico City.

The revolutionary climax

Calles controlled succeeding presidents until the election in 1934 of General Lázaro Cárdenas. The Cárdenas regime was notable for its assistance to the working class, greatly accelerated land distribution and agrarian reforms, freedom of speech, and, above all, the nationalization of the foreign-owned oil industry.

The Cárdenas presidency is generally seen to be the climax of the Revolution. This convulsion cost more than a million lives and caused great destruction yet also laid the foundation of national pride and identity.

▲ Francisco Madero, the first president of the Revolution era, was an unassuming and modest idealist. His brief period in office ended in a sordid betrayal and assassination.

▼ Pancho Villa and Emiliano Zapata, famous revolutionary heroes, met in Mexico City to discuss the struggle against Carranza's faction, which they considered too conservative.

▼ Thousands of women joined the revolutionary forces and fought as bravely as men. Adelita was a famous *soldadera*. A song about her is still sung everywhere in Mexico today.

▲ For thousands of peasants, the cry ''Land and liberty!'' meant leaving poverty-stricken homes to fight government troops. Many died in the merciless atrocities and massacres of their long struggle.

▶ General Plutarco Elías Calles was an able and effective president notable for his hostility to the Church. Using ruthless politics, he controlled the country for 10 years and ended decades of militarism.

▼ Pancho Villa was a bandit and outlaw. His hatred of oppressive governments developed his talents for leadership and revolt. Like Zapata, he was assassinated and became a legend in story and song.

▲ President Lázaro Cárdenas had a very personal style of government. His humanity and love of the land made him very popular. His nationalization of the oil industry was bitterly opposed by foreign owners, but it secured Mexico's future industrial development.

Modern Mexico

► "Make sure that the seed of culture germinates in Mexican soil" is the message of this poster. The alphabet letters being sown as seeds symbolize the importance of literacy in an advancing nation.

◄ These Mixtec Indians are waiting outside a clinic for medical treatment. Practical help like this is greatly needed in the Native American communities, where health care and education may not equal national standards.

▼ Luis Echeverría, who was president from 1970 to 1976, was a vigorous and outspoken Third World leader. His constant travels not only promoted Mexican trade but led to greater Latin American unity.

Population growth

Immense changes have occurred in Mexico in the 20th century. In 1900, Mexican society was headed by rich landowners, the masters of desperately poor peons working on huge haciendas and in the mines. The total population although growing, was less than 14 million.

Today, with more than 84 million people, the country has a substantial middle class. More than two-thirds of the population now lives in the cities— 13 million of them in the vast metropolis of the capital alone.

Such a rapid increase in population in a poor and war-shattered country created many problems. Some rural areas still do not have modern farming systems. Many Indian communities find it difficult to adopt new techniques. Young people leave their villages to seek work in the cities.

Persistent campaigns to improve agricultural output, as well as extensive land reclamation projects, have transformed deserts and jungles into thriving farms and ranches. Various government agencies have been formed to aid Native

◄ Electric power is so essential to Mexico's economic development that every effort is being made to extend power lines to all regions. A few sparsely populated desert areas still lack electrical service.

◄ In spite of the many benefits of Mexico's progress, the size and geographic obstacles of the country have created uneven stages of development. It has large dams and vast irrigation zones, but there are still areas without piped water, where rivers are used instead. Daily washing of clothes and bodies is an Indian tradition.

merican communities, providing them with schools, teachers, doctors, agricultural experts, and other services.

Cities that have grown very fast must cope with the influx of thousands of illiterate migrants from the villages, who live in shanty towns rife with disease and crime. Great efforts are being made to combat this social blight, but it will be a long and expensive struggle.

Prospects for the future

In the 1980s, Mexico began a program of industrial development that may bring long-term economic growth. Foreign companies have built many factories in Mexico, employing thousands of workers and boosting the local economy.

The country faces many challenges. A large number of its people live in poverty, and the population is growing much faster than new jobs are being created. Pollution and other forms of environmental damage are severe in some areas, especially in the densely populated Valley of Mexico and in industrial centers. Some elements within the government and army have been accused of repression and human-rights abuses. Yet Mexico has become a leading force in Latin American politics and development, a role that it will certainly continue to play in the 21st century.

▼ From Juarez, Mexicans hurry across the Rio Grande to the U.S. city of El Paso, Texas. They are entering the United States illegally—without proper permits and immigration procedures—in search of jobs. Each year, hundreds of thousands of illegal immigrants cross the border. If caught by the U.S. authorities, they are returned to Mexico.

▲ Carlos Salinas de Gortari became president in 1988. A native of Mexico-City, Salinas has pledged to ensure freedom of speech and other civil rights and to build a stable economy. In 1991 he visited the United States to discuss new trade and loan agreements between Mexico and its neighbor to the north.

Mexico City

Mexico City has a population of 10 million, and nearby Ciudad de Netzahualcóyotl, which was once part of Mexico City, houses another 3 million. All together, the metropolitan area around the capital has a population of more than 14 million.

The rapid growth of the city—caused mostly by people leaving the countryside in search of a better life—has caused problems. The services that provide water, electricity, housing, and sewage treatment cannot keep up with the rising population, and as a result the capital has extensive slums. But it also has well-preserved historic districts and striking contemporary architecture.

The Zócalo, an enormous open square, is the heart of the city. It stands over the original Aztec foundations of Tenochtitlán. The Cathedral dominates the plaza, its variety of architectural styles reflecting the 250 years it took to build. The National Palace rose from the rubble of Moctezuma's own palace and was first occupied in 1529 by Cortés. The Liberty Bell of the War of Independence hangs outside. The Bell is rung by the president on September 16 each year.

Colonial buildings

The old part of the city around the Zócalo has many Colonial churches and palaces, but some are sadly decayed and in need of restoration. The Basilica of Guadalupe is revered by Catholics as the holiest shrine of all the Americas. The site on which it was built was the scene of a miraculous vision of the Virgin Mary in 1531.

The beautiful old Colonial villages of San Angel and Coyoacán, now within the boundary of the city, have venerable cobbled streets lined with tranquil, colorful mansions and cottages. Some were built as homes for Cortés, Alvarado, and other Spanish conquistadores.

Elegant avenues

The Paseo de la Reforma, a magnificent tree-shaded avenue, leads to Chapultepec Castle, home of the ill-fated Emperor Maximilian. The park contains the Museum of Anthropology, acknowledged as one of the finest in the world. The long Avenida Insurgentes arrows through elegant suburbs and shopping centers.

▲ Tenochtitlán is pictured as it must have appeared to the amazed Spanish when they approached Lake Texcoco. Built among causeways and canals like Venice, its temples and pyramids were surrounded by markets and workshops. Archaeologists are still finding valuable remains of the Aztec capital under modern Mexico City.

▼ The heart of the city is the great Constitution Plaza, called the Zócalo. This was originally the center of the Aztec capital Tenochtitlán. The Zócalo is now dominated by the cathedral, which was begun in 1573 on the site of an earlier church built over an Aztec temple. The cathedral is a majestic building. The adjoining Sagrario Metropolitano is a separate church built in the 18th century.

▲ Like many cities, the Mexican capital has slums, with crowded tenements and desperately poor people. Many of those who live here have sought to escape the poverty of country villages, but their numbers are so great that jobs are difficult to find. These children appear happy enough, but their future may be hard and discouraging. The government sees the danger of excessive population concentration and is encouraging new industrial zones where work and homes are being created.

Places to visit in Mexico City

National Museum of Anthropology

Cathedral

Palace of Fine Arts

▲ Mexico City, one of the world's largest and fastest-growing capital cities.

Column of Independence

Chapultepec Park and Castle

▲ The Latin American Tower has floating foundation chambers to protect it from earthquake damage.

◄ Chapultepec Park is a beautiful expanse of woods, meadows, gardens, and lakes. An imposing castle in the park was the home of Emperor Maximilian.

Family life

The Mexican people have inherited the strong sense of family loyalty and kinship that characterizes both the Spanish and the Native American cultures. As a result, the family has always been the most important unit of Mexican society, although increased travel and migration, as well as other 20th-century changes, have somewhat weakened the traditional family bond.

Like most people of Spanish heritage, the Mexicans consider family to include grandparents, aunts, uncles, cousins, and even more distant relatives. Families and households are often large. The average family has three or four children, and other members of the family, such as grandparents or cousins, may share the home. It is common for young men and women to live in their parents' homes until they are married—and even after the marriage, if there is room. This is partly custom and partly brought about by the housing shortage.

Social activities center around the birthdays of family members and the religious holidays of the Roman Catholic calendar. Families who can afford it celebrate birthdays, weddings, and other family events with large parties for relatives and friends. Most Mexican families, however, seldom invite casual acquaintances to their homes; friends as well as business clients are generally entertained at restaurants or nightclubs.

The workday

Traditionally, lunch is the main meal of the day. Parents come home from work to eat it, and children often generally return home for lunch as well. In earlier times, lunch was often followed by a short nap, or *siesta,* during the hot midday; people would go back to work in midafternoon and work until well into the evening. This custom is falling out of use except in rural areas and small towns.

The favorite evening pastime of most Mexicans is television. Nearly three-quarters of all households have television, and almost all of them have radios. Movies are also popular, but videocassette recorders are much less common in Mexico than in the United States.

One aspect of family and work life that has changed greatly since the 1960s is the number of women who work. For centuries, women were regarded only as homemakers who took care of the house and the children, tended the family garden, and practiced crafts such as pottery or weaving. Women are now guaranteed equal employment rights under the constitution, and in recent years they have begun to enter the workforce. About 25 percent of Mexican women work outside the home, and the number increases every year. The difficulty of finding jobs and the scarcity of day-care facilities, however, keeps many women from seeking work.

Housing

Since 1938, Mexico has had a public housing program under which government agencies have built low-income housing for the burgeoning populations of cities and industrial centers. But the supply of houses and apartments falls far short of the need. Mexico City alone has about 1 million fewer housing units than its population requires.

Although most families prefer private homes to apartments, few lower- and middle-income Mexicans can afford to buy property. Large apartment complexes are therefore becoming more common and now ring the centers of all major cities.

▲ A Maya family in the Yucatan Peninsula. The Maya of today are the descendants of the Native Americans who built great pyramids and temples in the jungle centuries ago. Many contemporary Maya still speak the Maya language and follow traditional customs. They want to participate in Mexico's government and economy without losing their distinctive cultural identity.

▼ A family is photographed with men costumed as the Three Kings who attended the birth of Jesus Christ. Mexican families exchange holiday gifts on Three Kings Day, January 6, instead of Christmas Day.

▲ A family picnic. The dry and sunny climate encourages many people to spend a lot of time outdoors, and families often make weekend or holiday outings to a park or to the beach.

▲ A village in rural Mexico, where many dwellings lack clean water or indoor plumbing. If industrial production continues to grow, more rural villagers will probably move to the residential complexes being built around manufacturing centers.

Apartment buildings have been built in nd around every city, but more are needed. Mexico has a serious shortage of housing.

◄ The sound of corn being ground on stone plates called *metates* and the slapping sound of tortillas being shaped by hand have been part of Mexican life for thousands of years. Supermarkets selling prepared tortillas and other foods have made those sounds increasingly rare in the larger cities.

▲ Village women wash their laundry in a pool and spread it on bushes to dry. Although women are beginning to enter the workforce in greater numbers, many Mexican women work full-time as homemakers and mothers.

A religious society

Native religion and Christianity

Nearly 93 percent of Mexicans are Roman Catholics, followers of the faith that was brought to Mexico by the Spanish. The Church once wielded enormous power in the country, although the government has curbed its influence since Colonial days. Today many priests and nuns have taken on a new role, becoming spokespeople for the poor and oppressed.

Religion has been a fundamental part of Mexican culture for thousands of years. Christianity began with the Spanish Conquest, but it was grafted onto the base of existing religious practices. The Indians were better able to accept the new devotion at their old familiar shrines. Many of the early churches were founded on sites where the native gods had been worshipped, and the wiser Christian priests were able to convert the natives by allowing the new rites to continue in the place of the old.

Pre-conquest religious cults varied among the different Indian groups living throughout Mexico. They began with gods of elemental and peaceful aspect, but as the tribes became more aggressive and warriors ranked with priests, religion became linked with war.

The Rain God, Tlaloc, and the God of Wisdom, Quetzalcóatl, were joined by bloodthirsty deities demanding more and more sacrifices—usually prisoners of war. The temples of the Aztecs were piled high with corpses and skulls. Thousands of victims were sometimes sacrificed in a single day.

Not all the native people had such grisly rites, as their own gods never became so malignant.

Fiestas and churches

The Spanish word *fiesta* means feast-day, a religious holiday. In Mexico, local Saints and Virgins are worshipped and their anniversaries celebrated with much the same ritual that was used in the early days of Spanish rule. Some of these celebrations have become nationally famous and attract throngs of many thousands of devout pilgrims from all over the country.

▲ The Shrine of the Virgin of Guadalupe is the holiest in Mexico. Venerators of the Virgin crawl on their knees across the great plaza to worship at her miraculously painted image.

► Saints are carried on processional floats. To many Mexicans the richly garbed statues have a real and living compassion for the faithful. Men who carry the heavy images are extremely proud of the privilege.

The Virgin of Guadalupe, as Patroness of the Republic, has the place of honor in her Sanctuary in Mexico City. As in Spain, Holy Week is a time of devout religious spirit, with solemn processions and Passion plays culminating on Easter Day in joyful explosions of fireworks.

Many of the earlier churches clearly show how their Indian builders and craftsmen adapted their skills, merging the pagan with the new Christian religion. Richly decorated ornamental work created by the Indians included cunningly carved pagan figures and symbols among the gilded and painted angels and cherubs.

Many Catholic homes have their own imaginative and elaborate shrines. Weekly church attendance is dropping, but most people still attend church on holidays.

This Nativity play is being performed in the Shrine of the Virgin of the Remedies, Patroness of the Spanish, to whom prayers are offered for rain and cures for sickness. A conquistador brought her image from Spain.

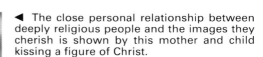

◄ The close personal relationship between deeply religious people and the images they cherish is shown by this mother and child kissing a figure of Christ.

▼ Passion plays are enacted in many towns and villages during Holy Week. The art and skill with which the various costumes are made reflect the national genius for handicrafts and the religious enthusiasm of the people.

Customs and festivals

▼ The annual September festival in honor of the Virgin of the Remedies is attended by many thousands of people. These gaily decorated towers are part of an old aqueduct that brought water to the revered sanctuary more than 350 years ago.

Fiestas and Saints

In many ways, Mexican life is still based on enduring religious beliefs. Its festival days are of Indian or Catholic origin. They all have a basic theme of adoration, whether of ancient deities or of the Virgins of Guadalupe and Remedios. Every village has its fiesta to honor the patron Saint's day, and times of drought and flood sometimes bring festivals in which prayers are offered for rain or sunshine.

The annual calendar of festival days contains nearly 100 important dates, but no one celebrates all of them. Some fiestas last for a week or more. They may be called *ferias,* or fairs, and include bullfights, cockfights, and agricultural shows with rodeos.

Fireworks

All fiestas culminate in firework displays after nightfall, when everybody surrounds the *castillo,* which is the set piece of an elaborately framed mass of fireworks towering above the eagerly waiting crowds. Equally exciting is the

▼ The ancient town of Tepotzotlán, 25 miles (40 km) from Mexico City, is famous for its lovely 400-year-old convent and church. Dedicated to St. Martin, it is the scene of many colorful festivals.

globo, a huge balloon of innumerabl tiny scraps of multicolored paper, hun with dozens of tiny lanterns. This floa slowly into the night sky until it catche fire and explodes in a brilliant ball c flames and flashing sparks.

The year of festivals all over Mexic begins properly with the Epiphany, th Day of the Kings, when presents are tra ditionally given. Carnival reigns over th week before Lent, and then comes Co pus Christi, memorable for the *Vola dores*—Dance of the Flying Men—a Papantla, near Veracruz. During thi traditional Indian dance, men swin through the air on ropes suspended fror a high platform.

Independence Day on September 16 i a time of national rejoicing. The presi dent rings Father Hidalgo's famous Lib erty Bell. All Saints' Day is an occasio for feasting. Also called the Day of th Dead, it involves celebrations in th cemeteries.

Some festivals and holidays	
Jan 1:	New Year's Day
Jan 6:	Day of the Kings—presents are given
Holy Week:	Processions, fiestas, and Passion plays
May 1:	Labor Day
May 3:	Masons and Builders Festival
May 5:	National holiday—anniversary of the Battle of Puebla
Corpus Christi:	Voladores at Papantla and processions in Mexico City
Sept 16:	Independence Day
Sept 30:	Commemoration of the birth of José María Morelos, one of the leaders in the independence movement
Oct 12:	Columbus Day
Nov 1–2:	Day of the Dead
Nov 20:	Holiday celebrating the Revolution
Dec 12:	Festival of Our Lady of Guadalupe
Dec 16–25:	Posadas and piñatas
Dec 25:	Christmas Day

Piñatas are pottery jars filled with presents or candy that are hung from above. As they swing freely, blindfolded children try to smash them open with a heavy stick. Everyone scrambles to catch the goodies as they cascade to the floor.

▲ Huejotzingo, near Puebla, is known for its Shrove Tuesday carnival commemorating the Mexican victory over French troops in 1862. Opposing forces take part in mock battles, ending with a spectacular explosion and deafening volleys of shots.

◀ Upper-class society in Mexico still includes families descended from Spanish grandees. Weddings and other family and social events are very formal ceremonies.

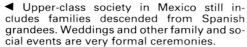

▼ Women praying at a death watch. Bereaved people believe that the souls of the departed remain close by and that the death watch ensures a safe passage for them. In spite of official opposition to the Church after the Revolution, the religious fervor of the people was not quenched.

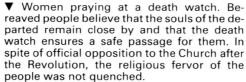

▲ Christmas Day in Mexico is preceded by the nine nights of *posadas,* when families and friends join after dark in processions commemorating the search of Mary and Joseph for room at an inn *(posada).* Dressed in Biblical costumes, they knock at neighbors' doors and are turned away. Only on the last night do they find a refuge; a party of thanksgiving is enjoyed by everyone at the house, which is chosen in advance.

Education

Mexico's educational achievements since the 1960s have been impressive. Educators have had to confront the problems of providing effective schooling to a rapidly growing population in which learning was traditionally confined to the upper classes. The challenge was made greater by the fact that many Native Americans do not speak Spanish, the official language of the country. Much has been accomplished, but much progress remains to be made.

The country's educational policy is aimed at providing each child with a primary education. Secondary schools, technical and vocational schools, colleges, and universities are also considered important, but the first goal is universal basic schooling, which should enable everyone to read and write.

The school systems are controlled by the states, except in the Federal District, where the schools are administered by the federal government. Each state is responsible for determining how best to meet the educational needs of its people.

Types of school
Kindergartens and nursery schools, like day-care centers for the children of working parents, are generally found only in the cities and larger towns. There are some private nursery schools, but most of them are quite expensive.

Primary school is free, and children are required by law to attend between the ages of 6 and 14. Attendance is far from universal, however, especially among children older than 10, many of whom leave school to help their families earn money. Classes are taught in Spanish, except in regions with a large concentration of Indian students; there Indian languages are used, although all students study Spanish. Many schools also teach English.

About 90 percent of all people over age 15 can read and write, although in many cases their skills are very limited. Since 1960, the government has established 12,000 literacy centers around the country to teach adults how to read and write. Illiteracy is higher in rural districts than in the cities. Other government-sponsored educational programs include worker training centers, mobile literacy programs that travel the countryside by van, and public reading rooms.

In 1989–90, Mexico had 14.7 million children attending 82,140 primary schools. There were 4.4 million students in 19,000 secondary schools and 2.2 million in vocational and teacher-training schools. About 1.8 million Mexicans were enrolled in the country's 80 colleges and universities.

The two largest universities are the National Autonomous University and the National Polytechnic University, both in Mexico City. Together they account for nearly half of all students who receive higher education. The National Autonomous University has the distinction of being the oldest university in North America; it was founded by King Charles V of Spain in 1551. The Polytechnic is more recent, having been founded in 1936. Other major universities include Iberoamericana University, a private university in Mexico City; Guadalajara University and the Autonomous University of Guadalajara, and the Autonomous University of Nuevo Leon.

Since the late 1960s, university students have emerged as a powerful, sometimes unpredictable political force in Mexico. Large-scale demonstrations by students in 1968 and 1987 prompted some reforms of political and educational policies.

▲ The nation's educational policy is focuse on improving primary schooling for all chi dren between the ages of 8 and 14. Adult lite acy is also a high priority.

▼ A strike by students at Mexico City's Na tional Autonomous University in 1987 shu down the university for several weeks. Th students were protesting new governmer educational policies, including stiffer admis sion standards.

▼ Traditional handicrafts are taught in special craft schools, many sponsored by the government. This girl practices woodworking in an open-air school in Chapultepec Park, Mexico City.

The government has devoted a significant percentage of the national budget to building new schools and modernizing old ones. All children, except in the most remote outlying regions, now have access to school.

▼ The National Autonomous University, despite being the oldest such institution in North America, has many contemporary buildings on its large campus. It is the country's largest, as well as its oldest, university.

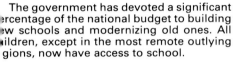

▲ A missionary school for the Tarahumara, a Native American people who live in northern Mexico. The Tarahumara are remarkable runners, both fast and enduring; the fastest among them can outrun deer, and the most enduring can cover hundreds of miles in a week. This school is run by the Jesuits, a missionary order of the Roman Catholic Church. Although education is no longer in the hands of the Church as it was in colonial times, some schools in rural areas are still run by the Jesuits.

The arts

Native artistic genius

The Spanish encouraged Indian painting and sculpture after the conquest, as they soon realized that the Native peoples had a highly developed natural gift for visual expression. Their frescoes, oil paintings, wood carvings, and masonry decorated the churches and monasteries that were built all over the country as the Spanish extended their domain. The art of fresco mural painting had been used in many pre-Columbian buildings, notably at the Maya temple of Bonampak. This tradition was spectacularly revived after the Revolution and continues its impact today.

During the Colonial period, most painting became stifled by European trends. But the awakening of a truly national artistic style began in the 1920s.

Revolutionary art

In 1921, an administrator named José Vasconcelos took over the newly created Ministry of Public Education and Fine Arts. His energy and encouragement shaped the careers of Mexico's three great muralists: Diego Rivera (1883–1957), José Clemente Orozco (1883–1949), and David Alfaro Siqueiros (1898–1974). Their artistic development was influenced by the political transformation of their country during the tumultuous years of revolution and reform in the early 20th century. Their paintings and sculptures expressed revolutionary ideals, including the dignity of humble laborers and the unity of people of all races.

Most of the work these muralists produced was commissioned by the state. Their murals were a type of social education—useful in a country where many people could not read. The last masterpiece of these great muralists was Siqueiros's enormous work *The March of Humanity*, a combination of painting and sculpture that rests on a huge turntable at a cultural center in Mexico City.

In addition to the social art of the murals, 20th century Mexico has produced abstract and landscape art. Contemporary works that draw on Native American folklore and pre-Columbian painting styles have come to be very highly regarded, as expressions of an enduring cultural heritage.

▲ Diego Rivera explored the riches of his country's history throughout his career and became one of its inspired interpreters. His murals in the National Palace are universally acclaimed for their flowing lines and color. This picture is a vision of his Indian world.

▼ This fine example of Siqueiros' work at the National University headquarters is a powerful symbol of teachers guiding a student to a future in which "his training will give fruit to the people who provide the seed." Siqueiros was a master of many technical innovations.

The chaotic and tragic themes of much of Orozco's work are superbly shown by his murals in the Hospital of Jesus, founded by Cortés in 1574. The artist is seen working on *The Four Horsemen of the Apocalypse,* a picture typical of his deep contempt for man's greed and cruelty.

Felix Candela, an engineering genius and architect, became famous for his extremely thin but strong parabolic shells of concrete. A brilliant sun creates striking contrasts of light and shadow at this fashionable Mexico City restaurant.

The Museum of Modern Art in Chapulpec Park contains the work of both Mexican nd foreign artists. This modern sculpture rembles a primitive Indian deity like those en at many pre-Columbian archaeological tes.

The beautiful baroque church of Santa aría Tonanzintla, near Puebla, is a wholly Inan concept of Christian glory. Dark-skinned ngels and cherubs are carved in a mass of wers and fruit, streaming forth in a dazzling aze of color.

Music, recreation, and sports

Mexico has many distinctive types of music and dance. Some of them are of Native American origin; others were introduced by the Spanish. Elements of ancient religious rituals have been preserved in a number of folkloric dances.

One type of song that has been popular for centuries is the *corrido,* a long, rhyming recitation with a simple melody. Corridos are often witty or satiric and may deal with politics, gossip, or the events of the day. They became especially popular during the Revolution, when they became a form of political journalism.

Mariachi bands are another feature of Mexican music based on the Spanish heritage. These strolling bands of musicians, usually dressed in elaborately decorated suits and tasseled sombreros, offer serenades of romantic songs and dance music. They are especially popular in Mexico City and Guadalajara.

Leisure and sports

Movies are a popular leisure-time activity. Mexicans enjoy both their own films and those produced in the United States. Many U.S. movies are filmed in Mexico; during the era when cowboy films were popular, American actor John Wayne spent much time working in the city of Durango. Mexicans who have made their mark in international cinema include actors Dolores del Rio, Jorge Negrete, and Mario Moreno (called Cantinflas) as well as Spanish-born director Luis Bunuel, who lived and worked in Mexico.

Rodeos and bullfights are regularly held in most cities and large towns. The rodeos, called *charreadas* after the *charros,* or cowboys, feature exhibitions of traditional Spanish-style horsemanship. Mexico City's bullfight arena, which seats 50,000, is one of the largest such arenas in the world. There are about 35 other bullfight arenas throughout the country.

Another spectator activity is the game of jai alai, which is called *pelota* in Mexico. Although the game originated in Europe, it is very similar to games played by the ancient Mayas and Aztecs. Players in a walled court use wicker scoops to catch and hurl a fast-moving rubber ball.

The most popular spectator sport in Mexico is undoubtedly soccer, which is called *futbol* there. Mexico City is a major site of international soccer competition, and big games draw more than 100,000 spectators. World Cup soccer matches were held in Mexico City's stadium in 1970 and 1986.

▲ The Dance of the Quetzal is seen its best in the south, where the ra streamer-tailed quetzal bird lives in the ju gles. This magnificent headdress represen its multi-colored feathers. In ancient time entire costumes were made of colored feat erwork by the Indians.

► The Ballet Folklorico has done much to preserve traditional Indian dances, using authentic costumes and music created through meticulous historical and archaeological research. Some dances are adapted to ballet, with choreography based on stories of the ancient gods and emperors.

▲ The Spanish brought bullfighting to Mexico when they established their immense cattle ranches in the north.

▼ Basketball owes its popularity to the neighboring United States.

▼ The Azteca Stadium in Mexico City holds 100,000 soccer fans. Seen here is a national match between Mexico and Colombia.

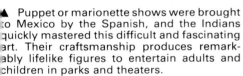

▲ Puppet or marionette shows were brought to Mexico by the Spanish, and the Indians quickly mastered this difficult and fascinating art. Their craftsmanship produces remarkably lifelike figures to entertain adults and children in parks and theaters.

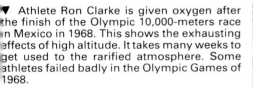

▼ Athlete Ron Clarke is given oxygen after the finish of the Olympic 10,000-meters race in Mexico in 1968. This shows the exhausting effects of high altitude. It takes many weeks to get used to the rarified atmosphere. Some athletes failed badly in the Olympic Games of 1968.

Food and drink

Traditional cooking

In recent years, Mexican food has become popular in many countries. Many restaurants in the United States and elsewhere feature Mexican dishes.

Eating Mexican style is an adventure and a delight. The highly piquant and pungent flavors have been enjoyed almost unchanged for centuries. Corn and beans have been basic ingredients since they were first cultivated in Mexico thousands of years ago. The dozens of varieties of chili peppers add their uniquely fiery flavor and are an important source of vitamins.

Regional variations

Many Mexicans states have their own regional specialities and styles of cooking. Puebla is the home of *mole poblana*, the national favorite, a dish of turkey simmered slowly with many spices, chocolate, chilies, and nuts. *Carne asada*, marinated strips of beef grilled with a peppery avocado, tomato, and garlic sauce, is popular in the northern cattle-raising states.

Bitter oranges are used for flavoring in Yucatan, where meat and fish are cooked wrapped in banana leaves. Seafood is at its best on the Gulf coast where restaurants in Veracruz serve succulent dishes of red snapper, snook bass, kingfish, and jumbo-sized shrimp.

Fruits and vegetables of every kind grow abundantly in Mexico's varied climate. Melons, tomatoes, and strawberries are now valuable export crops. The country is one of the leading producers of high-quality coffee, and its chocolate was first grown by Indians many hundreds of years ago.

Drinks for all tastes

Mexico's lager beers are popular. Cactus plantations produce a mildly alcoholic beverage called *pulque*, which is drunk mostly by the poorer folk. *Tequila* and *mescal* are two highly potent spirits distilled from a liquid extracted from cactus plants. They are traditionally drunk with salt and freshly squeezed limes.

▲ The patio of this converted old Colonial palace is now an outdoor restaurant.

Make yourself a Mexican meal

GUACAMOLE
2 large, ripe avocados
1 tablespoon finely chopped onion
2 teaspoons finely chopped chili pepper
1 tomato, peeled and chopped
1 tablespoon chopped fresh coriander
salt and pepper to taste

Peel the avocados and remove the stones. Mash the avocados into a pulp with a fork in a bowl. Then mix in the other ingredients carefully. Cover the guacamole with foil and place in a refrigerator until it is ready to be used. Serve it as a dip or with salad at the start of your meal.

PICADILLO
2 lbs minced beef
1 onion, chopped
1 clove garlic, chopped
3 tomatoes, peeled and chopped
2 cooking apples, peeled, cored, and chopped
3 chili peppers, washed and finely sliced
2 oz raisins
12 stuffed olives, sliced across
¼ teaspoon ground cinnamon
¼ teaspoon ground cloves
2 oz blanched, sliced almonds

3 tablespoons olive oil
salt and pepper to taste

Heat 2 tablespoons of olive oil in a heavy pan. Add the minced beef and stir until it is browned all over. Then add the onion and garlic and cook for a few minutes before adding all the other ingredients, except the almonds. Simmer for 30 minutes. In the meantime, heat the rest of the olive oil in a frying pan and add the almonds. Fry for a few minutes until they are golden. Add the almonds to the picadillo when it is cooked. Serve with rice.

CALABAZA ENMIELADA
3-lb piece of pumpkin (or squash) cut into six pieces
1 lb brown sugar
6 tablespoons of water
¼ pint whipped cream

Remove the seeds from the pumpkin or squash. Put the water in a shallow oven-proof dish and arrange the pieces of pumpkin in it. Sprinkle with the sugar and bring to a boil. Cover the dish and simmer for an hour, basting with the syrupy liquid every 15 minutes. When tender, allow to cool. Arrange the pumpkin in dishes, pour the syrup over it, and top with whipped cream.

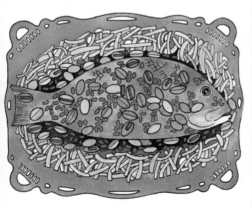

▲ Fruit grows so abundantly in Mexico that freshly squeezed juices are cheap and popular. Orange juice is the regular breakfast starter in many homes.

Regional dishes

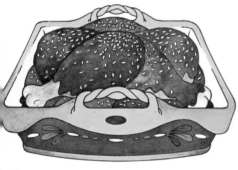

▲ Regarded as *the* national dish of Mexico, mole poblana's turkey is cooked with a sauce of over 30 ingredients, including chocolate.

▲ The warm seas surrounding Yucatan teem with exotic fish. These are cooked with savory spices in Creole style.

Tortilla fillings

Tortillas

Tomato sauce

Chili sauce

Chilies

Onions

Grated cheese

Chicken

Tortillas, tacos, enchiladas, and tamales are all made from corn and wheat flour. They are stuffed with variations of fillings based on those shown above. Tamales are steamed inside wrappers of corn or banana leaves, while the other three kinds of pancake are fried or baked.

◄ Maguey agave plantations are common in the dry central plateau. The liquid tapped from their hearts is made into the mildly alcoholic beverage called *pulque*.

▼ Street stalls like this are found in the poorer suburbs and in villages. Practically everything, including meat, is bought and sold on a day-to-day basis by the owner. Customers cannot afford to store food, so it is all sold freshly picked or killed.

Agriculture and rural life

▲ Mexico is one of the three major Arabica coffee producers in the world. These coffee beans drying on a patio floor are grown in the tropical south and may be destined for the growing export market.

▶ Corn has been the staple crop of Mexico for thousands of years and is often still harvested by hand on peasant-owned plots where mechanization would not be feasible.

▼ The potential for livestock production has only recently been properly understood. Traditional cattle-grazing areas in the dry northern pastures have very poor capacity; American-type feed lots like this now flourish in the rich grasslands around Veracruz.

The end of feudalism

Agriculture was one of the major reasons for the Revolution of 1910. At that time, 97 percent of the land was held by only 830 rich landowners. Another 2 percent belonged to half a million or more small farmers. The remaining 1 percent was *ejidos,* or group farms owned by communities.

This feudal system ended with the Revolution, when the state took control of the land. Much of it has been distributed to peasant farmers. Today nearly three-fourths of all farmland has come under ejidal ownership.

Livestock and crops

Mexico has abundant pastureland—nearly 40 percent of its total territory. Cattle-ranching is important, especially

in the north, where Hereford cattle and other specialty breeds are raised to produce high-grade beef for export. Sheep, goats, pigs, and chickens are raised almost everywhere.

Farming in many parts of the country depends upon irrigation, and since the 1930s Mexico has installed many large systems of dams and canals to make the most efficient use of its water, which is rather scarce everywhere except in the far south.

Corn is the main crop and the staple of the Mexican diet. Mexico grows enough corn, beans, rice, sugar cane, vegetables, and fruit to meet its needs and even to export considerable quantities of produce. Strawberries, grapes, melons, avocados, and tomatoes are the principal export crops. Agricultural economists are worried, however, that overcultivation of the land, combined with the growing population, could lead to a severe food shortage in the future.

Mexico has a large commercial fishing industry. The most important food species are shrimp, sardines, oysters, squid, abalone, mackerel, red snapper, and crabs. Most of the catch is consumed within the country, although the export market for Mexico's seafood is growing.

▼ Although many *peones* work on communal lands called *ejidos,* some manage to keep their own smallholdings, aided by local farm banks with low-interest loans.

A typical pastoral scene dominated by the
~~~owy crest of Popocatépetl. Many Mexican
~~~eep show their cross-bred descent from
~~~anish Manchego and Merino breeds.

Beautiful Lake Pátzcuaro in Michoacán is
~~~mous for its delicate white fish and the
~~~ique butterfly nets of its fishermen. These
~~~rasc Indians control their nets with a pole
~~~tween the "wings" so that they glide si-
~~~ntly under the fish.

The rapid growth of Mexico's population
~~~s made increased food production vital.
~~~echanization, irrigation, and fertilizers are
~~~nsforming backward rural areas into
~~~rmlands.

Commerce and industry

Mexico has a trade deficit, which means that it imports more goods than it exports. Economic planners are attempting to increase the amount of exports. Before about 1970, Mexico's exports consisted mostly of agricultural products. Now more than two-thirds of the value of all exports comes from crude petroleum.

Manufactured goods are also· exported; Mexico imports industrial raw materials, produces goods such as appliances, chemicals, and toys in its factories, and exports the finished products. The United States, Spain, and Japan are its leading customers. Many U.S. and European companies, especially auto manufacturers, operate plants in Mexico where workers assemble cars and other products for eventual sale in other markets.

Two industries that are closely related are crafts and tourism. Mexican artisans create a wide range of craftworks, including pottery, leatherwork, jewelry, and woodcarvings. A great many of these items are exported, but still more are sold in Mexico to the 6 million or so tourists who visit the country every year. The income from tourism and the new jobs created in hotels and restaurants are so important that Mexico has created new resort areas such as Cancun and Ixtapa to attract visitors.

Industrial development

The oil mining and refining industries are the largest sectors of the manufacturing economy in terms of earnings as well as number of employees. Iron and steel production, auto assembly, brewing and food processing, and paper manufacturing are also important components of the economy.

For centuries, Mexico has been one of the world's leading sources of silver. Mines that were worked by the Spanish conquistadors are still producing this metal. Gold, mercury, manganese, copper, zinc, and lead are also mined, as is coal. The country also has reserves of iron ore. In 1981, new deposits of gold,

silver, copper, and lead in the Baja Peninsula were discovered by a sensing device aboard the U.S. space shuttle *Columbia*. The radioactive substance uranium is mined in several states.

Mexican workers are represented by several large labor organizations. The Confederation of Mexican Workers was founded in 1936 and was an important political force through the 1970s. It has a women's branch called the Federation of Women's Labor Organizations. Since the late 1970s, the largest and most powerful labor union in the country has been the Union of Petroleum Workers, which represents the more than 80,000 employees of Pemex, the state-owned petroleum corporation.

▲ Toluca's Friday market is noted for nativ handicrafts like this pottery. Bought by Mexi cans for use at home and by tourists as souve nirs, craftware like this is made in scores o villages in the region.

▶ The art of gold and silversmiths reached a high level long before the arrival of the Spanish. Some centers such as Taxco have streets of metalsmiths' and jewelers' shops.

◀ Since the nationalization of oil in 1938, Pemex (Petróleos Mexicanos) has controlled all aspects of the oil industry. Pemex is one of the country's largest employers.

▼ An industrial worker in Jalisco state, on the Pacific coast. The government is trying to develop centers of industry and manufacturing away from the central valley around Mexico City, in order to distribute the population more evenly.

▲ Several variations of agave plants thrive in Mexico. These include henequen, the fibers of which are called sisal hemp. Yucatan is the leading producer of this raw material for ropes, mats, and hammocks.

▲ Pottery is one of the oldest crafts. In Mexico, potters have innumerable examples of their ancestors' work to emulate. The range is enormous, from objects in common use to beautifully painted decorative work. Apart from Talavera ware from Puebla, most of the best pottery comes from Indian villages.

Transportation and immigration

Mexico has the most modern and efficient road system in Latin America, with 146,300 miles (235,430 kilometers) of roads; about half are paved. Many of the roads have required blasting to clear a path through steep mountains or bridge building to carry traffic over deep gorges.

The Pan-American Highway, which runs from Alaska to South America, passes through 2,000 miles (3,200 kilometers) of western Mexico. Its biggest users are the drivers of the tractor-trailer trucks that are responsible for much of Mexico's transport.

Mexico City has an extensive subway system, and the country has a modern railroad network that is used primarily for carrying freight. Shipping is important along the coast; Veracruz and Tampico are the major ports. There are about 80 airports, of which nearly half offer international service.

Mexico also has a well-developed communications network. The press is particularly active in Mexico, which has 400 daily newspapers that represent a variety of political parties.

▲ Airstrips are essential in mountain and forest country where there are no roads. This landing ground is in Chiapas, a tropical state with many archaeological sites that are accessible only by air or by mule tracks. Pilots of these small planes develop great skill in tough conditions.

▼ Container trucks have to travel thousands of miles in blazing sunshine and must be able to carry large loads insulated from the tropical heat. The well-engineered main roads of Mexico enable these trucks to travel safely at high average speeds over long distances.

Immigrants

While some Mexicans leave their country to seek work in the United States, people from other Latin American countries are moving to Mexico to escape political persecution. Since 1983, Mexico has tightened its own border patrols in the south, hoping to control the number of refugees entering the country.

Refugees from Guatemala, south of Mexico, in a relocation camp in Chiapas state. Many Guatemalans, like many people in southern Mexico, are of Maya descent. These Indians are seeking political asylum.

▶ Horses are a common form of transport in Mexico today. They were first introduced by the Spanish when they conquered Mexico. The Indians were terrified of the horses at first, thinking they were gods.

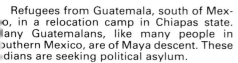

The wide main highways and city avenues enable heavy traffic to proceed swiftly and smoothly. American and German cars dominate the fast-growing automobile industry.

▼ An Aeroméxico plane takes on passengers and luggage in Mexico City. Formerly owned by the state, Aeroméxico is the country's largest airline.

Fast facts

Population figures are for 1989.

Official name: The United Mexican States

Area: 758,259 square miles (1,967,183 square kilometers)

Mountains: Sierra Madre Oriental, Sierra Madre Occidental

Highest point: Pico de Orizaba, or Citlaltepetl, 18,501 feet (5,639 meters)

Population: 84,275,000

Population density: 111 people per square mile (43 per square kilometer)

Population distribution: 70 percent urban, 30 percent rural

Capital: Mexico City (pop. 10 million)

Major cities: Ciudad Netzahualcóyotl, formerly part of Mexico City (pop. 3 million); Guadalajara (pop. 2 million); Monterrey (pop. 1.8 million)

Official language: Spanish

Religions: 92.6 percent Roman Catholic; 3.3 percent Protestant; 3.1 percent nonreligious; 0.1 percent Jewish

Ethnic groups: 55 percent mestizo (mixed race); 29 percent Native American; 15 percent white; 0.5 percent black; 0.5 percent other

Average life expectancy: 74 years for women, 68 years for men

Form of government: Federal republic with two legislative houses; 63 members in Senate, 500 members in Chamber of Deputies

Head of state: President

Local administration: 31 states, each with a governor and a state legislature, and a Federal District around the capital

Currency: Peso, divided into 100 centavos; approximately 2,600 pesos equalled $1 U.S. in 1990

Land use: 39 percent meadow and pasture, 23 percent forest, 13 percent farmland, 25 percent cities and other

Principal exports: Petroleum, automobiles and automobile parts, processed food and beverages

Principal imports: Machinery, chemical products, iron and steel, food

---

Chronology

5000 B.C. Settlement of Mexico's valleys and coastal plains begins.

1500 The Olmec culture develops around Veracruz; the Maya culture begins in the Yucatan Peninsula.

200 The Mexica people build a colossal city called Teotihuacan near the future site of Mexico City.

A.D. 400–900 The Maya civilization reaches its highest achievements in architecture and science.

856 The Toltec people build a ceremonial center at Tula.

1325 The Aztecs take over the valley of central Mexico and build Tenochtitlan on the future site of Mexico City.

1519 Spanish explorer Hernán Cortés lands in Mexico.

1520–21 The Aztec empire falls to Cortés and his men. Mexico becomes a Spanish colony.

1778 San Francisco, California, becomes the northern limit of Spanish rule in the American West.

1810 A priest named Miguel Hidalgo leads a rebellion against Spanish rule but is captured and killed.

1821 Agustin de Iturbide proclaims Mexico independent of Spain and makes himself emperor.

1824 Mexico's first president, Guadalupe Victoria, is elected.

1836 Texas secedes from Mexico after Mexican general Santa Anna is defeated by Texan soldiers.

1846–48 Mexico and the United States go to war. Mexico agrees to surrender half its territory to the United States.

1864–67 Mexico is an imperial state. Archduke Maximilian of Austria, supported by French troops, is emperor. The emperor is executed and the republic restored in 1867.

1876 Profirio Diaz takes power; his dictatorial rule sparks a peasant revolt.

1910–17 The Mexican Revolution, a civil war, brings democratic reforms and a new constitution.

1929 The Institutional Revolutionary Party (PRI) is formed.

1934 Lazaro Cardenas is elected president and speeds the pace of land reform and economic development.

1968 The Summer Olympic Games are held in Mexico City. Thousands of Mexican students demonstrate against political repression.

1988 Carlos Salinas is elected president.

1991 Salinas seeks new trade agreements with the United States and Canada.

Further reading

Adamson, David G. *The Ruins of Time: Four and a Half Centuries of Conquest and Discovery among the Maya.* New York: Praeger, 1975.

Augelli, John P., editor. *American Neighbors.* Grand Rapids, Mich.: Fideler Co., 1986.

Benson, Elizabeth P. *The Maya World.* New York: Crowell, 1977.

Berdan, Frances F. *The Aztecs.* New York: Chelsea House, 1989.

Casagrande, Louis B. *Focus on Mexico: Modern Life in an Ancient Land.* Minneapolis: Lerner Publications, 1986.

Catalano, Julie. *The Mexican Americans.* New York: Chelsea House, 1988.

Coe, Michael D. *The Maya.* New York: Thames and Hudson, 1987.

Covarrubias, Miguel. *Mexico South: The Isthmus of Tehuantepec.* London: Routledge, Chapman, Hall, 1986.

Diehl, Richard A. *Tula: The Toltec Capital of Ancient Mexico.* New York: Thames and Hudson, 1983.

Fincher, E.B. *Mexico and the United States: Their Linked Destinies.* New York: Harper Junior Books, 1983.

Irizarry, Carmen. *Passport to Mexico.* New York: Franklin Watts, 1987.

Kendall, Jonathan. *La Capital: The Biography of Mexico City.* New York: Random House, 1988.

Kennedy, John G. *The Tarahumara.* New York: Chelsea House, 1990.

Kurian, George. *Mexico and Latin America.* New York: Facts on File, 1990.

Metz, Leon Claire. *Border: The U.S.-Mexico Line.* El Paso, Tex.: Mangan Books, 1987.

Ochoa, George. *The Fall of Mexico City.* Englewood Cliffs, N.J.: Silver Burdett Press, 1989.

Odijk, Pamela. *The Aztecs.* Englewood Cliffs, N.J.: Silver Burdett Press, 1990.

————. *The Mayas.* Englewood Cliffs, N.J.: Silver Burdett Press, 1990.

Oster, Patrick. *The Mexicans: The Personal Portrait of a People.* New York: Morrow, 1989.

Perl, Lila. *Mexico: Crucible of the Americas.* New York: Morrow, 1978.

Reavis, Dick J. *Conversations with Moctezuma: Ancient Shadows over Modern Life in Mexico.* New York: Morrow, 1990.

Riding, Alan. *Distant Neighbors: Portrait of the Mexicans.* New York: Knopf, 1984.

Rodman, Selden. *A Short History of Mexico.* New York: Stein & Day, 1982.

Roper, Robert. *Mexico Days.* New York: Grove-Weidenfeld, 1989.

Rummel, Jack. *Mexico.* New York: Chelsea House, 1990.

Sabloff, Jeremy A. *The Cities of Ancient Mexico: Reconstructing a Lost World.* New York: Thames and Hudson, 1989.

Smith, Eileen L. *Mexico: Giant of the South.* Minneapolis: Dillon Press, 1983.

Stein, Conrad. *Mexico.* Chicago: Childrens Press, 1984.

Time-Life Books, editors of. *Mexico.* Alexandria, Va.: Time-Life Books, 1986.

Trout, Lawana Cooper. *The Maya.* New York: Chelsea House, 1991.

Wepman, Dennis. *Hernan Cortes.* New York: Chelsea House, 1986.

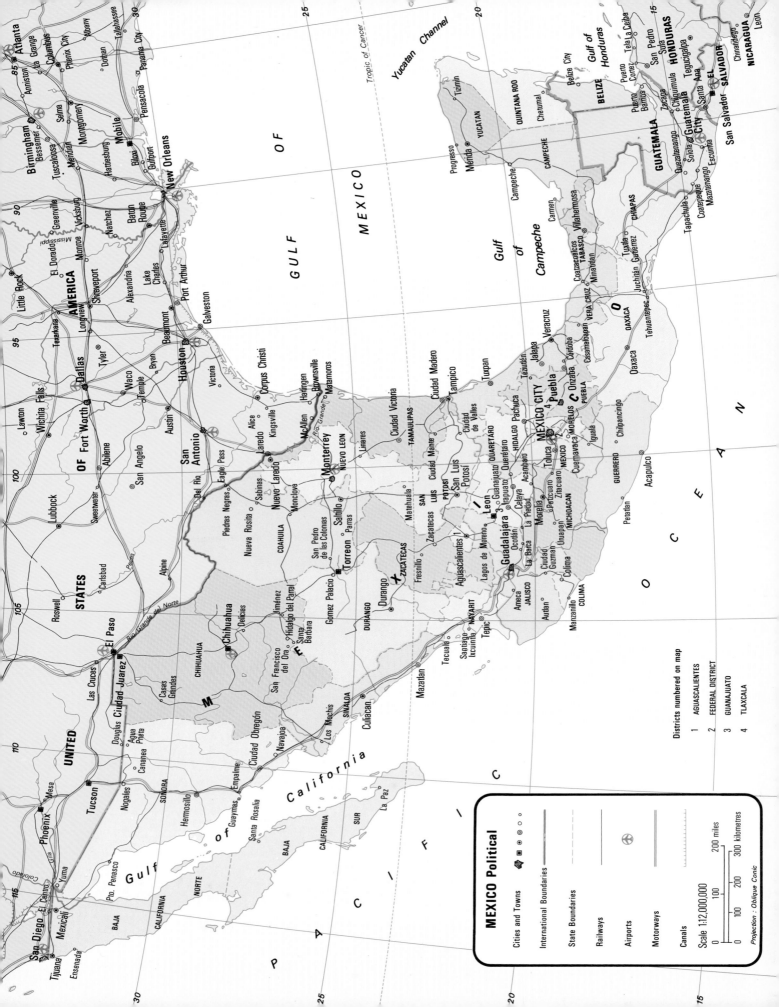

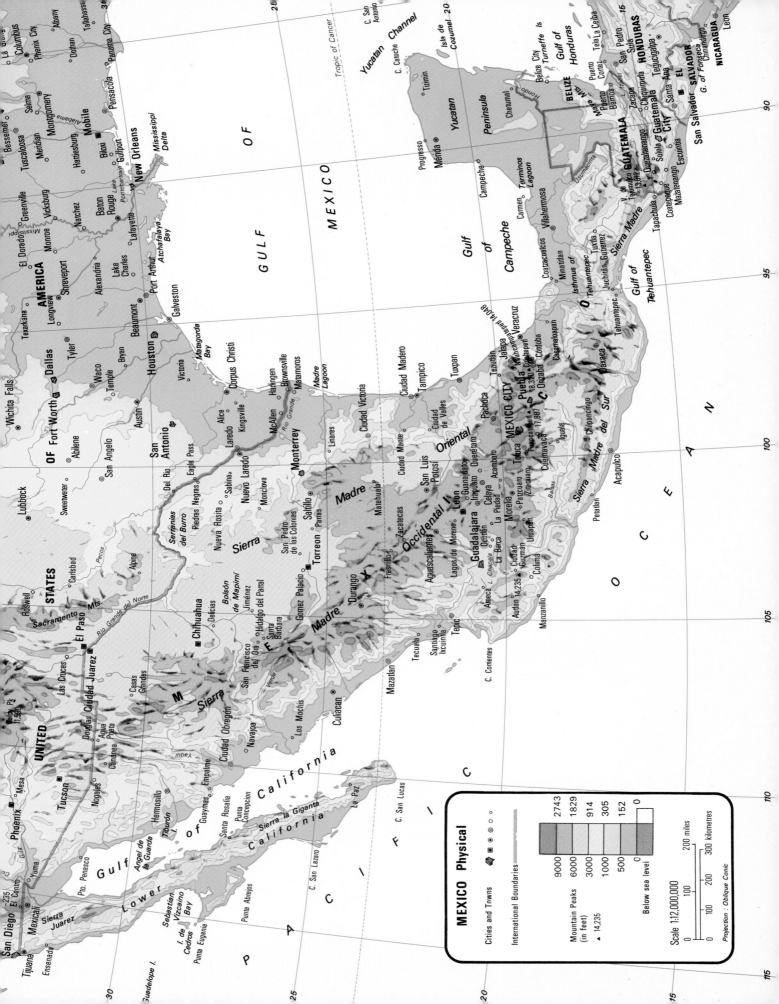

Index